UNDERCOVER CUSTOMER: 100 WAYS TO FIX YOUR BROKEN CUSTOMER SERVICE

By Sherron A. Stevens

This Book is Dedicated To April Stevens:

"Thanks mom for raising me with respect and work ethics which has gained me much success in the workforce and life. You made me who I am today, and I owe my abilities to your exceptional parenting skills!"

What is an Undercover Customer?

In my experiences working in the fast food industry, I sometimes felt as if I were an undercover customer. Although an employee, I was able to put myself in the customers' shoes and easily empathize with them.

This allowed me to enhance my own customer service skills and not only better serve my customers but also become a major influence to my co-workers and a complement to my managers.

So, I came up with the concept of "undercover customer." It is not only the title of my book, but also the name of my customer service consulting/training company that will help train employees and managers to develop exceptional customer service skills.

One of the services that my company provides is a customer service evaluation. How do I do this? By going into the business location and pretending to be a real customer. So, in fact, I am the "undercover customer."

Who Am I and Why Should You Listen to Me?

You may be wondering, "What does he know?" The truth is, there are many customer service books written but not always by people who have experience working directly with customer's everyday.

My name is Sherron Stevens and I am 18 years old. Many young people my age just want a job, but I truly enjoy working with customers. I have something to offer that most people just don't have these days -- exceptional customer service skills.

My first job was at the age of 16 at Chick-fil-A in Columbus, Ohio. To be perfectly honest, I only took the job to make money to buy some cool stuff. But once I started that job, I realized I was good with customers. I had the passion, the drive, and the ability to do exceptionally well at customer service. Little did I know how this job would impact my life.

Through my first year of working at Chick-fil-A, I received numerous feedback cards from customers, reference letters from managers and verbal compliments from co-workers and customers alike. Every week, these compliments all mentioned the same thing -- my phenomenal customer service.

   Chick-fil-A was a great stepping-stone for my career in customer service and customer relations. I eventually left

the job to move 30 miles away with my family. I was very comfortable with this job and my performance, but I didn't have the confidence that I could be successful anywhere else. I was wrong!

   My next job was at Donatos Pizza, also located in Columbus, Ohio. I worked hard each day and found out that my customer service skills worked here, too. Each week customers would tell me that I would do big things in life because of my strong work ethic and positive interaction skills with customers. All of these compliments eventually grabbed the attention of Jane Grote Abell, Chairwoman of Donatos Pizza in Columbus, Ohio. I was invited to be recognized in front of the whole company. This gave me the confidence that I have enough talent and knowledge in the customer service field to write a book on customer service.

How I Began My Book

I conducted my own study by visiting various restaurants, hotels and other businesses where customer service is a very important part of the job. I identified customer service practices among employees that represented what was both exceptional and poor in the customer service skill level at these businesses. I observed employee interaction with customers for several weeks and took notes. Unfortunately, I witnessed some very poor customer service at many businesses.

The result of my research is a book I created that will help you see where you can improve to make a huge difference in customer service. This book contains 100 tips that will improve your sales and in the long run, turn your entire business around. By following these tips, I am confident you will develop loyal, long-term customers.

This book focuses on customer service within minimum wage businesses. One expects and generally receives excellent customer service at very high-end establishments, but don't customers deserve good service from employees at minimum-wage businesses, too?

Further, a new survey from Citigroup and *Seventeen Magazine* found that almost 80 percent of students get a part-time job during the school year.

  These part-time jobs are in food, retail, hotels and etc. These jobs are usually designed for people without degrees, but they represent a huge number of people who work for major chains and companies that customers frequent every day. Employers need to recognize that these employees work directly with customers and can have a huge impact on how customers perceive the business -- and the chances that they will come back. Change the game by improving your customer service skills.

  Improving products plays a small part in satisfying a customer. What most companies do not focus enough on is good customer service. This is what keeps customers coming back. Follow every tip in this book and you will see a huge difference in customer loyalty, sales, and increased company profits.

What is Customer Service?

Customer service is responding to customer needs and expectations in a way that will make them have a memorable experience, motivated them to come back, and inspire them to tell others.

In this competitive world, business organizations must understand the importance of the customer and their place in the company's future growth. In other words, the future of the company is often in the hands of the customer. Shouldn't companies, therefore, put more effort into their business practices to attract and maintain customer loyalty?

The Underlying Issue With Customer Service

In order to know how to deliver good customer service, it is important to first understand why there is such a big problem with customer service today. First, employees and managers are not trained to have exceptional customer service skills. They are generally given an employee manual that tells them what to do and what not to do on their job.

However, there is no program in place that coaches these employees how to deliver customer service effectively. The domino effect results in each employee and manager with poor customer service skills showing others by example how not to treat customers. This creates a never-ending cycle of poor customer service skills throughout the company.

How Important Is Customer Service?

A number of studies reveal the importance of customer service. One example is The Ross Business School at the University of Michigan, which rates some 240 companies across 34 industries on a monthly basis. These ratings are more about the customer service provided by employees and less about customers being satisfied by a product/service.

The average rating is 76.9. In high school or college, this grade would be considered a "C." Just average. The airline industry has a 67 percent rating, the equivalent of a "D+." Retail is rated a 78 percent, which is a C average. These numbers alone prove that companies are performing just average or below when it comes to customer service. How can companies expect to receive the highest customer service ratings when their employees are doing so poorly in serving their customers?

So, how important is customer service? VERY important!

Surprising Customer Service Statistics

Below is research conducted on Customer Service:

70 percent of buying experiences are based on how the customer feels they are being treated. *(Source: www.mckinsey.com)*

80 percent of companies say they have superior customer service, but only 8 percent of their customers agree that these companies actually have superior service. *(Source: www.leeresources.com)*

Almost 9 out of 10 consumers say they would pay more to ensure superior customer service. *(Source: Customer Experience Impact Report by Harris Interactive/Right 2010)*

More Surprising Customer Service Statistics

86 percent of customers stop doing business with certain companies based on their customer service experience.
(Source: Customer Experience Impact Report by Harris Interactive/Right 2010)

Americans tell an average of 9 people about good experiences and an average of 16 people about poor experiences with businesses. *(Source: American Express Customer Survey, 2011)*

In a 2010 E-tailing Group , only **10 of 100** online merchants made the cut for stellar customer service. (Source: Annual mystery shopping study by the E-Tailing Group, 2010)

***Why Customer Service is Everybody's Responsibility ***

According to the *International Journal of Business and Commerce*, customer service is the key to how successful a business is. In today's increasingly competitive environment, quality service and customer satisfaction are critical to corporate organizations. Delivering high quality service is linked to increased profits and corporate image. Customer satisfaction is the route to sustained high performance.

Organizations should be aware of the fact that customer dissatisfaction sends customers straight to the competition and leads to long-term losses. Ensuring quality customer service is everybody's business in the organization. However, it is the responsibility of top management to create an environment that fosters customer-oriented services in a customer-oriented organization.

#1- Show Some Cheese

That's right, I'm talking about showing them your cheese! Not the cheese in your fridge, but that great big smile of yours. Customers want to walk into a store and feel welcome. A simple smile will do that.

Frowning or grumpy employees can intimidate customers and make them walk right out the door and down the street to your competitor.

If you're smiling till it hurts, you're doing it right. A co-worker of mine once said, "After working for five hours and smiling, I feel like my face is stuck." We just laughed and did some more smiling.

#2-Talk it Out

We all talk to our friends. That's how we get to know each other. Right?

Talk to your customers. Talking is a way for two people to open up and be comfortable with each other. Talking with the customer helps them feel comfortable enough to ask you questions about your products/services.

#3-Speak Up/Speak Clearly

Customers are often short on time and patience, so it's important to speak loud (well, not too loud) and clear. Customer should not have to continuously ask you to repeat what you said.

Make sure you speak slow enough, loud enough and clearly enough so the customer gets a good understanding of what you are saying. A customer can get irritated if they can't hear you or don't understand you. It starts the conversation on an awkward step that can down quickly.

#4- Don't be a Robot

Speaking loudly and clearly doesn't mean you have to sound like a robot. Speak enthusiastically as if this is the best product/service you have to offer. People tend to enjoy you if you sound excited.

Speaking with enthusiasm gives you more credibility as a sales person and makes the customer feel more encouraged when it comes to purchasing.

#5- Show that Crease

It's the 21st Century and we have something called an iron to unwrinkle clothes. Your appearance on the job is very important. You never want to come to work with wrinkled clothes.

Employees who don't care about their appearance also send a message to their customers that they don't care about their job or the customers. Don't be careless about your appearance. Show the crease!

#6-Flutter Those Lashes

Genuine smiles can be detected not just with the mouth but with your eyes. Use your eyes as a tool to say "hello". Eye contact has been proven to be one of the most effective ways to send a message.

When you make eye contact with a customer, it appears that you are interested in them and this will influence them to show interest in what you have to offer. It also makes them feel welcome in your place of business.

#7- Find Out What the Customer Wants

Don't just assume you know what your customer wants; you could be wrong and end up wasting their time and patience.

You can learn what customers want and what they like by listening and asking questions. Customers will appreciate that you care for their feedback on the products/services.

Finding out what customers like and want is also a good way to tell what's trending and what's not trending with your products/services. Customers will appreciate the feedback, and it's also a way for the company to upsell on the not-so-popular items.

#8 Pay it Forward

Many employees are afraid to ask the customer if they need any additional help. If you see a customer that needs help, such as an elderly person or mother with children, offer to help them with things like carrying their bags, taking their food out and/or reaching for higher items in a store.

A customer will be both appreciative and impressed if they see that you are willing to help them without an additional charge. Be willing to drop what you're doing to help customers.

#9- Show Your Gratitude!

The customer walked away and you didn't say thank you? Unacceptable! Always thank the customer for their business. Without customers, you have no business and no place to work.

It's very simple. Without customers, there are no sales, no money and no job. You should never be too busy to tell a customer two simple words: "Thank you." They'll appreciate your taking time to thank them for their business and will most likely come back.

#10- Be In sight

You pop up out of no where and the customer says "Oh, there you are!." A customer should NEVER have to look for you. Always be readily available or have someone readily available to help the customer.

There is nothing more frustrating than for a customer to have to find someone to help them. It sends the message that they aren't important and that you aren't interested in their business. Chances are, too, that this customer will not return.

#11- Watch Your Mouth

Are you enjoying the rest of your food from lunch or chomping down on that yummy minty gum? You might be enjoying yourself, but to the customer, it looks extremely unprofessional.

The problem with gum chewing is that some employees will chew on gum like a cow and even pop it. How annoying to customers! This also includes having food in your mouth while serving a customer. This is distracting and rude to a customer and very unprofessional. So, watch your mouth!

#12- Watch Your Conduct

You represent the company you work for even when you are on break. Most people have cell phones, but never ever use them while working unless it is an emergency.

Likewise, while on break, keep it professional. You might think it's OK to talk on the phone at a restaurant while on break, but no one wants to hear your conversations with your husband or kids or how annoying another employee is, especially if it is a customer who recognizes you.

Always use proper etiquette and conduct in public. You never know who might be seeing or hearing you, including customers! Go outside or somewhere quiet to talk.

#13- If You Don't Know, Find Out!

When you don't know an answer to a question, don't just say, "I don't know." That's not what customers want to hear and it will sound like you don't really care to help them.

If you don't know, go and find the answer from an employee or manager who does. The customer will recognize that you're really trying to help them and that you value their business.

#14- Promote the Promos

We live in a tight economy where budgets are small and people tend to watch how they spend their money.

Make sure you are upfront with customers on extra costs involved in services or products. And be sure to always let them know about your free promotional items. Customers love the word "free" and will appreciate your letting them know about special offers and pricing in effect. And you can be sure they will tell their friends about it, too!

#15- Watch Your Mouth - Again

Cursing may be acceptable in some circles, but it is never acceptable when you are in the presence of customers. It's not cool and it makes you look very unprofessional.

When a customer hears employees cursing, it makes a customer feel that the whole place of business is unprofessional. Customers want to eat and shop in a respectful environment, especially if they bring their children.

#16- Say My Name, Say My Name

We've all heard the Beyonce song, "Say My Name" and even sung along to it. She has a point there. The point is that you should learn and say the customer's name. Why? Because it establishes a personal connection with the customer.

When a store employee remembers the customer's name, it makes the customer feel important. They are no longer just a customer but someone whom the store considers important. It makes customers feel special. This special tip is very often what creates customer loyalty and a decision by the customers that this is the only place of business where they want to frequent.

#17- Be a Problem Solver

When you see a customer is upset, you need to run! Okay, maybe not run, but walk fast and take action quickly to solve the problem. Take a proactive approach when it comes to solving customer problems and complaints.

Things can go wrong, but the key is how you fix it for the customer. Find a solution that will satisfy the customer. This really shows that you care about the quality of your products/services, and about them. Let them see that you're doing everything in your power to make sure they have an exceptional experience.

#18-Don't Keep'em Waiting

Picture this: the store is full of customers waiting in line for a long period of time, they are getting irritated and their kids are getting cranky, and all you see looking out at the crowd of customers are angry faces.

You have lots of people to help but you think to yourself, "I can't possibly help everyone at once." You're right, you can't help everyone at once but you can let people in line know one simple thing. Try this: "Hello everyone, I do apologize about the wait in line, we are more then happy to help you and are going as fast as we can. We will be with you shortly."

This doesn't solve everything, but it at least lets the customer know the reason that they're waiting. When people have a reason, they respect it and patiently wait.

#19- Own up to Your Mistakes!

First of all, let's get one thing straight. No one is perfect, and it is never too late to apologize! This is very important to customer satisfaction. Anytime something is messed up, you need to apologize, even if it isn't your mistake. This lets the customer know that you are sorry about their bad experience.

Apologizing lets people know that you are also not happy with the service/product they were offered and you intend to fix the problem. They need to know you are on their side. They will be likely to come back to your place of business.

#20- Give your best, Give the best!

"Wow, that's great," is one of the greatest compliments you can hear from a customer. It shows you have gone the extra mile to make sure everything you give to a customer completely upholds to your standards. You want to ONLY serve the best.

If a customer is familiar with your product/service, and you have given them your best, they will enjoy it and come back for more. Think about it. As a customer yourself, if you like something, you'll continue coming back.

With that being said, if your product/service is bad, then you are not upholding the standards. This could ruin a customers experience and they may not want to come back. So, always give THE best and give YOUR best.

#21- Put Yourself in the Customer's Shoes!

We've all heard this a thousand times, but how many of us actually use it? Putting yourself in the customer's shoes means relating to them through similar experiences of your own.

For example, you may see customers struggling with small children or customers who appear to be having a bad day, and other customers who are just plain grumpy. Their problem is now your problem, but remember you have no doubt been there yourself.

Don't jump to conclusions about your customers; you don't know their personal circumstances. They may have just gone through a divorce, or have financial or family problems. Often, a kind word and calm demeanor can actually soften them. Remain professional and helpful, giving them the benefit of the doubt. Treat them as you would want to be treated and you may be very surprised at the results you get.

#22- Have a Customer Appreciation Day

Customers love to feel like they matter and are appreciated by the stores they frequent. What better way to show your customers how much you appreciate them than by having a Customer Appreciation Day, right? It's an effective way to say Thank You to your customers.

How often to have Customer Appreciation days is up to each business but it should include discounts on products/services, discount coupons, and other specials only offered on this special day. Have a drawing for free products. Your customers will come and bring their friends and will tell others about how great this place of business is.

It's also an occasion to market your customer service skills. Remember to say Thank You and show genuine appreciation for the customers. They will show their appreciation by coming back.

#23 – It's The Little Things That Matter

Little things may often go unnoticed by employees and managers, but they usually are quickly noticed by customers. Customers expect the big things, like good product, fair price, and excellent service, but they will judge you, too, by the little things.

What are those little things? It could be anything from a messy service area and employees who seem to be confused and disoriented, to confusing check-out and return aisles. Remember, although your product and services may be tops, customers want their entire shopping experience to be memorable.

A good way to check how you are doing on the little things is to periodically walk through your place of business as a customer, looking for little things that may annoy you. In addition to a walk, also try calling your place of business as a customer. If you are being put on hold for long periods of time or greeted with a rude employee, that is not a little thing.

#24 – Be A Good Coach

Everyone has a boss, but not everyone has a coach. What's the difference? A boss is someone you work for, but a coach is someone you work with. A coach is someone who leads the way and shows you how to do it.

Coaching is a skill that will produce more effective and successful employees. Coaching is leading by example, not just telling you what to do. A good coach will continue to train and guide you, gives you useful feedback, and recognition for good performance.

Be a good coach to your employees and you will see the difference in the quality of service they deliver to your customers.

#25- Ask Open-Ended Questions

Change the way you ask customers questions. "How may I help you?" is a good open-ended question that will stimulate conversation, not just a yes or no response. You can also try these: "Hello, what can I help you find?" or "How can I make your shopping easier today?" These are all good questions that can make a huge difference and a lasting impression on the customer.

#26- Slow down, Partner

When you're delivering customer service, remember you are helping customers find what they want, not auctioning off your products/services. You don't want to talk so fast that the customer doesn't understand what you're saying.

Clarity is important when it comes to customer service. Customers need time to absorb what you're saying so they can fully grasp what services/products you are offering. This creates a mutual understanding.

#27- Clean As You Go

Clean is just as important at work as it is at home. In fact, it should be in everybody's job description. Why? Because customers like to shop at a clean place of business. This includes clean bedding in hotels, clean floors and tables at restaurants, and clean carpeting and aisles in stores.

No one likes to clean, but here's a way to make it easier. Clean as you go. What do I mean? If you see a customer spill a drink in a restaurant or observe dust and dirt at a retail store, clean it up. Don't wait. A customer wants to eat, sleep and breathe in a clean and safe environment. Clean as you go instead of saving it for later will make the job easier and make the business always shine. "Save it for later" often means you're not going to get to it any time soon. Customers will always return to a clean place of business.

#28- Unfunk the Funk

Speaking of clean, we all know sometimes your place of business can have some funky odors. Make sure you are always aware of how something smells. This is especially important for places of business like hotel rooms and restaurants. Unpleasant odors can quickly turn customers away.

Smells are important to a customer. If something smells good, it signals to the customer that the place of business is clean and the employee cares not only about their business but their customers, too. Fresheners are also OK but make sure they are not overpowering.

#29- No Bashing Allowed

"OMG that customer was obnoxious." How often have you said that about a customer after they have left? But can you be sure they didn't hear you or read your lips? In addition, your attitude and negative thoughts can easily show through in your behavior toward them.

In addition, negative words about customers can quickly pass along to others inside the organization. This creates a negative environment that can be seen by the customer. Keep the environment positive and free of all customer bashing -- no matter how difficult the customer is.

#30- Take Interest in the Customer!

Customers like employees who take an interest in them. Sometimes, they even find the need to vent. Maybe they are having a bad day and just need someone to listen to them.

You may think this is not part of your job, but by simply asking a customer about their day and listening to them will establish good rapport by making them feel appreciated and important. Of course, be sure you do not pass any personal information on to other employees. This would ruin the customer's trust in you.

#31-Provide a Wow Experience

Wow! Such a basic word but it means a lot. Your brand is more than just a slogan or logo. It represents what your company stands for. You need to create memorable experiences for the customer.

Do what other companies aren't doing. Create an exceptional experience for the guest so they can brag about your place of business. Give them the WOW factor -- not just good customer service but exceptional customer service. It will quickly set you apart from the competition and is a powerful way to market your company.

#32- Convert Them into Fans

You have two types of customers, those who regularly come to your place of business and those who are just stopping by to browse. You have the power to convert the newbies into fans.

A fan is an enthusiastic and loyal customer. While it's very important to keep your regular customers happy with consistent exceptional service, it's also very important to turn those newbies into fans. You need to pay special attention to those who are new to your products/services and take the time to tell them about how good your product/services are. If a customer has never been to your place of business, they're not familiar with what you offer. So take the time and effort to convert browsers into loyal shoppers.

#33-Respect your Elders

Older customers create a unique opportunity to become loyal shoppers if you treat them with respect. I know you've heard this before but it is critical for all employees to understand the importance of respecting elders.

It's important to slow down and listen. Elderly people have been around longer and have tons of life experience. They know what they want. Listen and treat them with respect by saying yes ma'am/sir and no ma'am/sir. In a world where manners are almost nonexistent, this creates exceptional customer service. All customers, including your elders, will notice how respectful you are and will come back.

#34-Get it Right the First Time

How do you get it right the first time? By asking questions. At first, asking customers questions can make you feel uncomfortable, but what is even more uncomfortable is for a customer to get the wrong product/service.

Asking the customer questions shows you care about them enough to ensure they get the right product/service from you. If you don't understand what they're saying, just ask them. It's as simple as that. Customers will be happier when you ask questions and get it right the first time than asking no questions and being completely wrong.

#35- Show That You Care, Even After the Sale

Some may believe their job is done once the sale is complete. But good customer service will also be concerned about how satisfied the customer is after the sale. Next time you see your customer, ask them how they liked the product/service. It's good feedback to ensure your product/service was exceptional.

It really shows that you care when you follow up with the customer to see how they liked your product/service. A customer feels that you care about their business. A completely satisfied customer is much more likely to walk through your doors again and again.

#36-Don't Lie

Lying is bad to begin with, so don't do it. Don't even stretch the truth to a customer, telling them something you don't actually know is a fact or promising them something you really can't do. Sooner or later, it will come back and bite you.

Customers expect you to tell the truth and are quick to pick up when you are lying. In most cases, they will not give you a second chance. Customers rely on what you tell them, so only speak what you know to be truth. If you don't know the answer, don't just make something up. Go find an answer and always be truthful.

#37- Check Your Attitude

Everyone has a bad day sometimes, but never take it out on your customer. They can detect when you are annoyed or frustrated with things at work and/or maybe even things outside of work.

Non-verbal signals such as heavy sighing and rolling the eyes will be quickly picked up by a customer. This may make the customer think that they are causing you problems. It can make them feel uncomfortable to the point where they never want to do business with you again.

Everyone has a bad day, but always check your attitude at the door.

#38- Keep'em White

There's nothing like someone smiling at you and talking to you with bad breath. It is very disrespectful to a customer when you have bad breath. Personal hygiene is very important when it comes to customer service.

Avoid smelly foods like onions and garlic right before you go on the job, and always brush your teeth and use mouthwash so you are always fresh and presentable to your customers. You never want to chase away your customers or prevent them from asking you questions about your product/service because of your personal hygiene.

#39- Keep it Fresh

We all get super busy at work and eventually we all end up sweating. Sweating can make you smell unpleasant, and this is not good for customers who are around you all day.

Shower well and use deodorant, even take a fresh shirt with you to work, just in case. Remember, your appearance is how the customers will judge your place of business. So, keep it fresh and clean, just the way customers expect.

#40- Don't Be Too Hol(e)y!

Piercings may be popular in today's society but it has no place in a professional setting. Sorry. It just doesn't fit.

Piercings are commonly accepted by the younger generation, but not by all culture groups. Don't take a chance on offending customers. Piercings can easily stereotype you as a person your customer does not want to do business with. You don't want to be stereotyped as unprofessional.

Take earrings out before work or think twice before getting pierced at all. Piercings can not only affect jobs at the minimum-wage level but also prevent you from getting higher-end jobs in the future.

#41- Cover Up Those Tats

Tattoos are also very popular among both men and women in today's society. But tattoos may offend customers from different cultural and/or religious backgrounds.

In order to prevent any customer from being offended or feeling uncomfortable with your tattoos, it is best to cover up your tattoos before going to work.

#42- Clip Those Tips

Our hands and fingers touch many things throughout the day and is also one of the first things that customers may notice about you. That's why you always want to make sure your hands and fingernails are squeaky clean, even underneath the nails.

Customers who see that your hands or nails are dirty will tend to question the cleanliness of a place of business. This is especially true of customers at restaurants since your hands come in close contact with their food!

#43- Pull up Those Trousers

Full moons can be nice to view at night but customers don't want to look at your full moon at your place of business. Sagging pants that reveal half your underwear is very, very unprofessional.

If you want your customers to take you seriously, please use a belt and pull up your pants. The sagging pants look is disrespectful to customers.

#44- Stay Right There

We've all had busy days where there is more to do than there is time to do it. But each customer deserves your full attention.

Make sure you have fully addressed your customer's needs before you walk away, especially if they are still talking. Make sure you have answered all their questions before you end the conversation.

#45- Be Clear to Staff

Speaking clearly and being understood is just as important for managers as it is to customer service personnel. Managers need to be clear to staff on performance expectations.

Unclear information results in bad information being passed on from one staff member to the next, resulting in confusion, a lack of organization and mistakes within the business. How does this affect customers? They can clearly see when a place of business is or is not being run efficiently. No customer wants to shop at a very disorganized store or restaurant.

#46-Tell Them What Ya Want!

Providing valuable feedback to employees is an effective way for employees to continue improving. No one can improve if they don't know what they're doing wrong.

Managers need to make sure they are constantly giving feedback so employees are clear on exactly where they need to improve. This directly affects customer service, and you can be sure that your customers will notice and be very pleased.

#47- Put That Phone Away!

Your cellphone is not a toy, especially at work. Put that phone away and focus on the customer. Your job is to create a memorable experience for them. When you are on your phone, it appears to the customer that they are not important. They will not feel connected to your place of business.

#48- Stock it Up

Keeping shelves fully stocked should always be part of your job. You want to be able to grab an item off the shelf quickly when a customer requests it. Don't make them wait until you search the warehouse for the item that should have been right on the shelf.

Stocking is a good filler job and needs to be done regularly. If you're doing your job, you're stocking to the top. You want to always make sure that everything in your place of business is stocked. For example, if you sell fries, make sure ketchup is stocked. If you work at a hotel, make sure you have towels stocked. Customers get annoyed when they have to stop their busy schedule to come and ask you for something that should have already been stocked and ready to go.

#49 - Seek First To Understand

Listening is a skill. There is listening, which is just hearing words, and then there is active listening where you really hear what customers are telling you.

The difference, in the eyes of the customer, is that by actively listening, you are able to clearly understand and respond to the customers needs in a way that will completely satisfy them.

So, seek first to understand by listening carefully.

#50- Learn to Upsell

People today tend to watch what they buy, but they are not always aware of complementary items to their purchase. This where you come in by "upselling."

Upselling means recommending to customers or asking customers if they would be interested in adding a product/service to their order. An example might be offering them extra filters when they purchase a new coffee pot, or extra bags when they buy a new vacuum sweeper.

A customer can either accept or not, but they will appreciate the offer. Upselling shows customers you are going the extra mile to make sure they have everything they need on their shopping trip and are fully aware of all their options.

#51-Don't Pester Customers

There is an art to being accommodating to customers and being annoying. Being accommodating would be to ask the customer if you can help them find something. If the customer says "no," they probably are still browsing.

The difference would be if you continue to ask the customer if they need help after they already told you no. That is pestering the customer and very annoying.

When customers say "no" quickly, it usually means "no, I'm not interested at all." If a customer says "hmm no", you can possibly try one more time. After that, stop asking them questions but stick close by to help them if they need you. Don't pester them into buying your product/service. It may be the last time you sell them anything!

#52 - The Importance of Repeat Customers

Finding new customers is a much harder process than keeping current customers. But make no mistake; repeat customers are extremely important to business and should be taken seriously.

Treat your existing customers as new customers. This means not slacking off but giving them the same value and consistency in products and service that you would with new customers.

Longevity in customers means a steady stream of sales, so never underestimate the power of repeat business.

#53 - Good Is Not Good Enough

When it comes to customer service, keep your standards high. In fact, keep your goals slightly higher than what you think you can do.

Why? Raising the bar gives employees a challenging goal to reach for, and once they reach that goal, they realize that they are capable of more.

Vince Lombardi once said, "If we chase perfection, we can catch excellence." Raising the bar on customer service goals may not reach perfection but it will certainly make a huge difference with your customers and your business.

#54-Show Them Policy 4783294

Every store has policies, which are the things employees can and cannot do for customers. If a customer asks for something that is against policy, take the time to explain the policies with the customer. Explaining the reason for store polices helps the customer feel comfortable with your place of business.

In addition, try to offer something else to the customer instead. Don't just say "No, I can't do that." Follow up immediately with something you CAN do for them. This builds the customers knowledge about your product/service and also demonstrates that you are interested in making them a happy customer.

#55-Make Sure Your Website Is Accurate

More and more customers are shopping online these days, so it it critical to keep your web site up-to-date -- especially if you are selling products online or offering coupons. Directions and phone number information should also be accurate and up-to-date.

Every customer's time should be considered valuable. Wasting their time with wrong information on your web site can irritate them and send them right to your competitors.

Let's say a customer finds a coupon on the web site and they go to your place of business to find out that the coupon has expired, or applies to a different promotion. If this happens, find a manager and do something else for the customer. The customer came, expecting to get a deal, so offer them something equal of value. Then make sure you correct your web site.

#56- Introduce Yourself

Do your customers know you by name? Well they should. This makes a customer feel comfortable with coming to your place of business.

A name is a personal connection, and customers like it when they can be on a first-name basis with you. They need to know what type of people you are, and introducing yourself by name will go a long way toward customers building trust in your products/services.

#57- Don't Leave Them Hanging

A phone call from a customer is no different than a customer who is right in front of you at the store. They both deserve your attention. A customer who calls is showing interest in your products/services. If you keep them waiting too long, they may hang up and never choose your place of business.

If you must say, "Can you please hold," make sure you give a reasonable timeframe. You might also ask if they prefer you call them back. If the answer is yes, make sure you do call them back promptly. These calls need to be a priority.

#58- Don't Argue

"The customer is always right" is somewhat of a true statement. Even if customers are absolutely wrong, don't try and prove to them why they're wrong. You will never win this argument but will lose the customer.

Proving a customer wrong is not worth losing a sale. Give the customer the benefit of the doubt and you ultimately win because you kept a sale.

#59- Offer Product Information

Most customers want product information before they buy the product. This is especially true when it comes to nutritional products. After all, these products are going directly into their body.

For example, a customer indicates they work out and seriously watch their calorie intake. Whether you run a restaurant or nutrition store, you need to have nutrient guides readily available to give to customers who are interested in calories and/or ingredients of your products. A customer will feel comfortable returning to your place of business because they feel you are knowledgeable which makes them more comfortable buying from you.

#60- Take Allergies Seriously

Customers can have serious health issues and allergies to certain foods. If your business is food-related, you need to be aware of product information and take allergies seriously. Allergies can create a life or death situation.

Most customers know what they are allergic to, so you, in turn, better know what's in your food or products. They are relying on you to give them accurate information. A customer needs to feel comfortable when ordering from you when it comes to their health. If they feel you are not taking their allergies seriously, you may lose a sale or worse, cause harm to a customer. Take allergies seriously and know what's in your products that customers could be allergic to.

#61-Be Specific

If you tell a customer that their product/service will be ready at a certain time, make sure that timeframe is accurate. Accuracy in product delivery times is one way to build credibility with your business. Customers will eventually have faith that you will deliver when you said you would.

#62- Compliment a Customer

When was the last time you complimented a customer? If you can't remember, it's been too long. Everyone likes to receive a compliment, especially customers.

Be sincere. Find something about your customer that deserves a good compliment. It could be their clothing, distinctive eyewear, great handbag or even the sound of their voice. It will brighten your customer's day and they will be sure to remember you.

#63-Treat Employees As Customers

Employees purchase your products/services too, so treat them as you would a customer. Treating employees with respect will create a welcoming work environment where the employees practice what they preach to all customers, including other employees.

#64- Choose The Right Time

You may have exciting news to tell the customer about choosing your new product/service which is great, but make sure you choose the right time. If you see a customer is busy, in a rush and/or has impatient small children, this is not the right time for a sales pitch, no matter how exciting it is.

Choosing the right time to tell the customer about product or store information ensures that you will have their full attention and they are receptive and able to actually focus on what you are offering. Otherwise, you risk annoying the customer if all they want at that particular time is for you to get their order done right and fast.

#65-Pull Them Aside

Don't ever give criticism to a co-worker in front of customers or other employees. This will embarrass the employee and make them feel uncomfortable. No one appreciates being given criticism when others are watching. This makes an employee feel inferior.

If you have to deliver criticism, pull them aside and deliver it privately. You want to give criticism in a way that will make the employee feel more empowered, not humiliated. They will be far more receptive, and you will have ensured that your employee maintains a positive attitude and demeanor toward customers following the conversation.

#66 - Tell Them Why

If you really want to get employees on your side, tell them why. It's human nature for people to support an issue if they understand the reasons behind it.

Take the time during employee training, and whenever a new policy or procedure is being implemented, to explain to employees why this is being done. Many policies are directly related to customer service, and you will find that your customer service will improve if employees are on your side.

#67- Don't Bash Your Products

Selling products to customers should be based on their particular needs and likes, not yours. Even if you don't like the product, keep your personal opinions to yourself.

Instead of telling the customer, "I don't like that at all," say something like, "I've had that one before; however, I prefer this one because...". A customer should feel they can choose what they want. So, point out the features and benefits and then let them decide. Don't make the customer feel pressured into choosing something they really didn't want. It's their choice, not yours.

#68- Do Not Discriminate

Discrimination comes in all forms, including race/color, age, religion, gender, disability, nationality and more. Discrimination in any form is strictly prohibited in business. You need to treat all customers equally. It's not only the law but your responsibility to customers. They are respecting your place of business by choosing your products/services, so show them the same respect!

#69- Don't Rush a Customer

"Okay, is that all?" is a statement you should never use with customers. It might sound to a customer that you are rushing them, and no one likes to be pressured. Take your time and the customer will be happy you took the time to make them feel important.

Try saying something like this, "Are there any additional services/products you would like to see today?" The customer will not feel rushed but completely satisfied with their shopping experience.

#70- Show Them How To Do It

One way to get employees on your side is to be willing to do what you are asking them to do. So, don't just tell them but SHOW them.

For example, if you have advice on their customer service skills, be able to show them the proper way to do it. If they observe your willingness to comply with company policies, they will be more willing to follow, too.

A customer, too, respects the place of business when they see someone from the team stepping up and helping out an employee. This shows professionalism and teamwork to the customer.

#71- Train Employees

Customer service is both a talent and a skill. Everyone has their own style when it comes to customer service. So, when training employees in customer service, don't insist on one particular style. If it has to be done your way, they may choose not do it.

You need to show those employees how they can use their natural talents to develop exceptional customer service skills. Telling them what you expect is not inspirational. Find something that makes that employee inspired and use that as training for them. Employees that are comfortable with customer service will likely do it exceptionally well.

#72- Clean that Porta Potty

I'm sure you don't have an actual porta potty in your place of business, but it may smell like one. One of the most important places to clean and keep cleaned are the bathrooms. If a bathroom is dirty, it gives a bad impression of your business. Customers will not feel comfortable in a dirty place of business, especially the bathrooms.

#73- Take All Forms Of Payment

It's good customer service to accept all major forms of payment. Credit cards, debit cards, cash and any other major credit cards should be accepted. Accepting only one or two credit cards is a major inconvenience if a customer only has one form of payment and it's not the one your place of business accepts.

You never know what credit cards customers are going to use. Offering several will go a long way toward making shopping easy and convenient for customers and not losing sales.

#74- Make Employees WANT To Come To Work

Work is work, but can you really make your employees want to come to work? If so, how? By making their jobs something they look forward to when coming to work.

Employees have opinions on what is important for them to enjoy their jobs, so ask them! Ask them if they are satisfied. If they are not satisfied, what can you do to make it better? Do they desire to move into another position at your place of business? You don't know unless you ask.

The truth is that if an employee is not satisfied, it will be seen by customers through that employee's body language. This can cause an employee to have bad customer service, when in reality, their real issue is that they are in the wrong job.

#75- Don't Give a Chore List

Employee chore lists are long and boring and can be tedious. Don't give an employee too many tasks at once or you will have them so focused on getting their chores done that their customer service will suffer.

When you put too much pressure on an employee, it interferes with their customer service skills. They rush the customer so they can get back to their assigned chore lists. Keep chore lists reasonable so employees have plenty of time to also spend with customers.

#76- Suit Up

Make sure you follow your company's uniform or dress policy. Why do companies have dress codes? It shows solidarity, unity and professionalism. It also shows customers that you are a team. For example, would a professional basketball team all wear different jerseys? No, it would not show them as a team working together. The same principle applies to businesses.

#77- Get Your Team Involved

There is a saying that "if it ain't broke, don't fix it." When it comes to customer service, no one is closer to your customers than your employees.

Involve your employees in any new program and ask their opinion before you implement something that will affect customers. Ask your team before you change anything. Some effective ways to obtain this information is through employee surveys or group meetings where everyone is allowed to contribute.

#78- Provide Incentives For Employees

Every work environment has some competition. Competition is often good to boost production and achievement, as long as the incentives are available to every employee.

Good incentives are those that offer rewards or awards to employees who work hard. Incentives can be given to individuals or even teams. An incentive gives the employee something to work hard for and makes them stand out as a goal setter and achiever. Customers will likely see the employees working hard in a business that offers incentives.

#79- How To Deal With Difficult Customers

There are entire books written on this subject: how to deal with difficult customers. You know the type. No matter what you do, they are not happy. Have patience. Take this as an opportunity to show the customer what your place of business has to offer. The customer knows most of the time when they're being difficult and sometimes even apologize. But how you treat them during this difficult time will decide how the customer views you.

As an employee who has to serve difficult customers, you will set yourself apart when you say something like "That's perfectly fine, take your time. We will get this right together." This makes you and the customer work as a team to get their order of your products/services right.

#80-Have Feedback Cards

Customer feedback is key to fixing and improving your place of business. It gives customers an opportunity to tell you, anonymously, what they like and dislike about your company. In turn, you can use this information to improve on areas that are weak and keep on doing what you are already good at.

Customer feedback cards are one of the most beneficial sources of customer information for a company.

#81- Offer Your Knowledge

You are smarter than you think. In fact, we all have knowledge and different perspectives to contribute to the conversation. Don't be afraid to share that knowledge with your customers.

When conversing with a customer, you both have an opportunity to share what you know on the topic. It can be related to your product/services or to something else of mutual interest. The point is that this type of interchange is good customer service. It creates an atmosphere of empowerment for the customer, and an important sense of connection. Customer service is more than just selling; it's about connecting with the customer.

#82- Speak English Please

When speaking with customers, speak in language that is common to everyday customers. New words and expressions should only be used if it's commonly understood by customers.

If you said this to a customer, "Yo bro, which hood you came from doe...." that customer may not only not understand what you're talking about but could also be offended. Always use everyday/common words that can easily be understood by any customer. Save all the new, hip talk for your friends.

#83- Don't Chat Too Much

Chatting among co-workers is fine, but don't be such a chatter box that you ignore customers. They will quickly turn and leave, and you will lose a sale.

Focus your time on the customer first, and then engage the co-worker in conversation after you have completely taken care of the customer.

#84- Don't Bash The Business

A customer may ask you how do you like working at this place. What you NEVER want to tell them are negative comments. It makes the company look bad, and it makes you look bad, too. In addition, a customer may start to second-guess your place of business if they see you are willing to do the same thing.

Bashing the business does nothing but damage to the business, the employee, and the customer. You don't have to lie, but you can certainly point out all the good reasons why you chose to work at this place of business. The customer will be reinforced that they, too, have made a good choice.

#85-Be Confident

You just offered your customer an additional product/service and you feel great. Then all of a sudden, the customer says "You're just trying to upsell me". Your mind goes blank and you see your sales pitch go down in flames. What do you do?

You need to be confident and let the customer know that you are offering them an additional product/service because it complements their previous purchase, or it's a good value as a promotional product/service and you would love to show it to them. When a customer sees you are confident, they will be more likely to say yes.

#86- Solve Work-Related Problems

"I just want to punch my co-worker right in the nose." You may not have actually said this but you may have thought it. Sooner or later, most employees have disagreements. You need to be able to solve them.

Problems with co-workers need to be resolved quickly. If not, they will escalate and affect your ability to work well with customers. If you are having a problem with a co-worker and it causes tension, this will more than likely spill over and affect your demeanor with customers.

Take the initiative to solve problems like an adult by taking the person aside and speaking to them calmly about the problem. You don't have to be their best friend but you have to work with them as a team. Customer know when you and another employee don't get along. Don't put your customers in an awkward position. Solve work-related problems immediately.

#87-Be Available and Open

You've heard that expression, "Happy wife, happy life." It's similar with an employer-employee relationship. Take time out of your busy day to talk with your employees. Listening to them and take what they say seriously.

Happy employees are productive employees. They are also much more likely to treat customers well. Keep employees happy and they will keep your customers happy.

#88- Don't Count the Minute

You stand there watching as you only have one minute left on the clock and then BOOM! It's time to clock out, but your place of business just got busy. Don't be an employee who abandons ship when you are needed most.

Your work team will appreciate the fact that you are stepping up to help out even though it's time for you to go home. Stay for an extra few minutes and help out. Your co-workers will be more likely to do the same for you. Helping each other creates a teamwork environment, which overall affects customers, too. The customers can clearly see when there is a team effort to help service them.

#89- Set Up for Success

Customers or co-workers don't like whiners. So, stop complaining about what you don't like and what you hate doing. This type of 'stinkin' thinkin' will negatively affect your potential outcome for success.

Thinking negatively becomes a habit and it brings down the team. Set yourself up for success by thinking positively, setting goals and achieving them. You will find that your whole outlook and demeanor will change for the better, and both co-workers and customers will notice.

#90- Learn from the past

"I coulda, shoulda, woulda .." is helpful when improving, but if you dwell too much on the past, it will affect your customer service skills. Learn from your mistakes and move on. We all make mistakes, but the key is to learn from them and use them as opportunities to do better.

#91- Keep Learning

Never think you know it all. Learning is a life-long effort. Learn as much as you can about your job and your business, as well as your customer. Be willing to learn from anyone and everyone, including managers, co-workers, employees and customers. Observe, watch, listen and learn.

What does this have to do with customer service? Knowledge makes you much more useful to customers. Customers like to do business with knowledgeable companies.

#92- Open On Time

No customer wants to come to your place of business to see the doors have not yet been opened. Especially if it's a big sale day! If you say you're open at 6am, make sure the doors are unlocked at 5:59am. Don't make your customers wait. It's rude, unprofessional and quite frankly, makes customers angry. Also, to the customer, you are not following your own policies. So open when it's time to open!

#93- Close Up Shop on Time

This is often a problem with small business owners. Sometimes they choose to close shop early. What they don't realize is that there may be a customer who is on their way to your place of business only to find you just closed shop. Do you think they will come back? Probably not.

Close shop at the scheduled time. If your place of business closes at 8pm, don't refuse to wait on a customer who comes in your door at 8pm. Just think, that last customer could make your profit goal for the day. A last minute customer will get very upset if you close earlier than your scheduled time or shut the door in their face and tell them you're closed.

#94- Be Bill Gates

Not all customers have the technology level of Bill Gates, nor should you expect them to. Not everyone understands technology. Your job is to help them with any technology difficulties they may have in your place of business and/or online. Take some time and give them a tutorial so they can use it next time. A customer will be glad that you stepped up and helped them learn something new.

#95- No First-Class Treatment

Sometimes customers may ask for discounts that are not advertised. First, find out if they qualify for discounts or programs. If they are not, say something like "I do apologize, but we are not offering any discounts at this time." Then be sure to let them know of upcoming discounts they may be interested in and qualify for. The customer may be disappointed that they didn't get a discount that day, but they will respect that you adhered to company policy and did your job properly.

#96- Turn That Ish Off

Many places of business have music playing in the store. But customers do not like going into a professional place to hear songs with curse words or other lyrics that are inappropriate and can offend. If your place of business decides to play music, ask yourself "Can this offend anyone?" If the answer is yes or you have even the smallest doubt, the music is probably not appropriate.

The customer needs and wants to be comfortable in order to come back. Make sure you don't drive them away with inappropriate music.

#97- Be a Rubber Band

What is a rubber band? Flexible! Every place of business has that one employee that calls off regularly. This places the burden on others to fill in for them. Be flexible, like a rubber band, and be available whenever possible to step up to the plate and help out. Your may even have to work in an area of the company that you may not like and/or are not comfortable with. Don't complain. Suck it up and help out.

Customers won't know that you are filling in. All they will see is a team running smoothly.

Tip #98- Open doors

What a great gesture it is to open a door for a customer. If you see customers that may have their hands full, or a customer in a wheel chair, open up the door for them. Small things like this go a long way. A customer will feel overjoyed and welcomed because you stopped what you were doing to come help them out for a few seconds. This shows your place of business has character. And, it's the right thing to do.

#99- Be Happy, Don't Worry

Honestly, this is a tip that can help your customer service overall. Come to your job and work hard every day. Be a symbol of success. Ignore the negative and just be happy. Don't worry about Negative things that may come your way. If you are happy and enthusiastic, this attitude will rub off on the team. This in turn will rub off on customers. Pretty soon, your entire place of business will stand out.

#100- Treat Them as a Guest

Throughout this book, I've been referring to customers by saying customer this, customer that. But aren't customers really like guests? When you use the word customer, you may just think of them as sales and making money. When you use the word guest, you think of someone who is here temporarily, and someone you would like to come back.

As a guest, you want to provide them with everything to make them feel at home. So, treat your customers as a guest in your place of business and they will always want to come back!!

MY CUSTOMER SERVICE SKILLS ACCOLADES

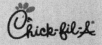

Chick-fil-A of Market at East Broad

6240 East Broad Street
Columbus, OH 43213
Phone: 614-631-2300
Fax: 614-631-2301

Dear Sir or Madam,

Sherron Stevens has been a part of our team for nearly six months. In that brief time, he has demonstrated his ability to serve our customers well. Our dining guests consistently go out of their way to notify the managers of how his personal service adds to their experience at Chick-Fil-A. He has received numerous C.A.R.E. comment cards regarding his genuine kindness.

As a young person working a new job, Sherron has demonstrated a willingness to learn as much as he can in all areas of Front Line Service. His generosity in assisting others has earned him respect among our team. Sherron's genuine positive attitude shines not only with the guests but also with fellow employees.

As he continues to develop in his career choices, I would recommend Sherron for any position which allows him to work closely with clients. He possesses qualities that would be valuable in any work environment where service is the foundation.

Sincerely,

Yolanda Dallas
Manager
Chick-Fil-A 02545

This is a letter of commendation from one of my managers at Chick-fil-A referencing my consistent willingness to go out of my way to help customers and how my service adds to the overall customer experience.

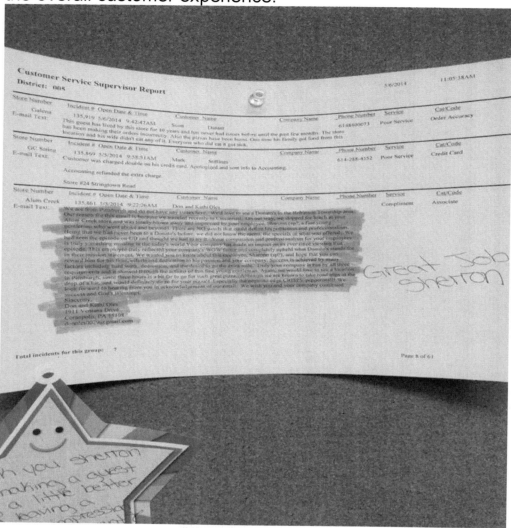

This customer was very impressed with my politeness and professionalism. The customer stated that I represented the company's "WOW" factor and standards. The customer also appreciated my dedication and desire to go the extra mile.

Market at East Broad FSU

From:	Chick-fil-A CARES <chickfilacares@na.ko.com>
Sent:	Tuesday, March 26, 2013 9:57 AM
To:	Market at East Broad FSU
Cc:	CFA Cares; David Rissier; Kim McGrady
Subject:	Priority 3-Capture / Sync Report # 3907789 / Colu
Categories:	Karen

Subject:

Priority 3-Capture / Sync Report # 3907789 / Columbus - OH - Market of East Broad FSU

Message Body:

This is a Priority 3 issue. There is no closeout necessary through Chick-fil-A CARES and no guest card was sent. Thank you!

Customer Comments: I was very impressed with Sherron Stevens. Infact I as so impressed I made sure I took his nam down and saved it on my iPhone. Sherron was extremely polite and went around to every table making sure everyon had what they needed. He madeconversation with the guests and made sure the place was clean. It was such a surpr to get this fantastic service and I want you to know that I will definitely make it a point to visit chik fil a more often because of him. Thank you Sherron!!!!

Customer Information:

First Name:	Esther
Last Name:	D'souza
Visit Frequency:	
Primary Phone:	(740) 8810007
Alternate Phone:	
Email Address:	Cdsouzabiz@aol.com
Street Address:	9040 ESIN CT
City:	POWELL
State:	OH
Zip:	43065-9047

Sync Record Information:

Email Date and Time:	03/25/2013 09:58:48 PM
Date Visited:	03/20/2013
Time Visited:	06:00:00 PM

This is an email sent to my jobs owner from a customer who appreciated that I paid so much attention to each customer's need. The customer was so impressed with getting such good customer service in a fast-food restaurant that she wrote down my name. She said she would return because of me.

This customer complimented me on my customer service and was so impressed that she decided she would come back to this place of business. This is exactly how you should make a customer feel!

Jane Grote Abell is the chairwoman of the biggest pizza chain in Columbus, Ohio. She had this to say about my future.

"I know you are destined to do great things in life" -Jane Grote Abell

    The gold pin in the photo was given to me by Jane -- a high honor that shows I upheld the company's standards. This day showed me how hard work and delivering good customer service has impacted customers, and it grabbed the attention by a top corporate executive. I left the meeting that day motivated to keep working hard and stay focused on what I do best -- making customers happy.

MY COMPANY

This book can and will change the face of customer service, and you can be the portal of change at your workplace if you follow the tips outlined in this book. It will bring your customers back for more. I use these 100 tips myself and have had much success. Follow these tips and you, too, will go far and rise above the competition.

In addition to writing this book, I have also started my very own customer service training/evaluation company called.... you guess it, Undercover Customer.

Please visit my company's web site at www.undercovercustomer.com to learn about our what we do. We offer many services including evaluations of your company's customer service policies, and also employee training.